101 Gourmet cupcakes IN 10 MINUTES

WENDY PAUL

101 Gourmet

cupcakes

IN 10 MINUTES

WENDY PAUL

FRONT TABLE BOOKS
SPRINGVILLE, UTAH

Text © 2011 by Wendy L. Paul
Photographs © 2011 by Marielle Hayes

ISBN: 978-1-59955-935-3

Published by Front Table Books, an imprint of Cedar Fort, Inc., 2373 W. 700 S., Springville, UT 84663
Distributed by Cedar Fort, Inc., www.cedarfort.com

THE LIBRARY OF CONGRESS HAS CATALOGED THE SOFT COVER
EDITION OF 101 CUPCAKES AS FOLLOWS
    Paul, Wendy.
        101 gourmet cupcakes in 10 minutes / Wendy Paul.
            p. cm.
        ISBN 978-1-59955-259-0 (acid-free paper)
        1. Cupcakes. I. Title. II. Title: One hundred one gourmet cupcakes in ten
    minutes. III. Title: One hundred and one gourmet cupcakes in ten minutes.

    TX771.P377 2009
    641.8'653--dc22

                                        2009006650

Cover and page design by Angela D. Olsen
Cover design © 2011 by Lyle Mortimer
Edited by Kimiko M. Hammari and Heidi Doxey

Printed in China

10 9 8 7 6 5 4

Printed on acid-free paper

Dedication

Contents

Small Cakes *with* Big Ideas

I HAVE ALWAYS LOVED spending time in the kitchen, creating new and delicious recipes. Many friends and family members call me and ask for recipes, so I decided to write them down and make a cookbook. Cupcakes are a perfect dessert, party theme, gift, get-well favor, or "just because I love you" treat. So my idea is thinking outside the box. Why not make a special cupcake with the convenience of using a cake mix? I know what you're thinking: "Will it taste homemade?" You bet!

BY USING THE RECIPES and time-saving ideas in this book, your cupcakes will look and taste like you slaved away the entire afternoon creating these little masterpieces. Go ahead and dust your face with a little flour to get the recognition you deserve. I won't say a word. Your family and friends will thank you for the wonderful creation you have hand made and home baked.

ENJOY THE CUPCAKE WALK!

—Wendy L. Paul

Tips for Success

MOST CUPCAKE RECIPES average closer to 18 cupcakes rather than 24 when baked. Be prepared. When using fillers such as candy and cookies, the batter will make closer to 24 cupcakes. When making the cupcakes in this book, the batter will be thicker than usual.

WHEN MAKING THE chocolate ganache, if the chocolate hasn't melted after putting the hot cream over it, place it in the microwave and cook on medium heat for 30 seconds. Stir again until chocolate is smooth.

IF YOU DESIRE to make several kinds of cupcakes with one cake mix, here's the trick: Make batter without adding flavoring. Separate batter into equal portions—let's say three—and then divide other ingredient amounts by ⅓. For example, chocolate almond, chocolate zucchini, and chocolate cream would all work well because they have a similar batter base.

SHAPED CUPCAKE TINS are available in round, heart, star, and square. You can usually find them in the cake decorating aisle at your local grocery store. Specialized tins are a great way to mix things up without a lot of extra cost.

DON'T BE AFRAID to mix and match frostings with different cake bases. Make the cake that your family will enjoy!

CUPCAKES WITH CREAM FROSTING or filling will need to be refrigerated after being baked and frosted. They can last up to one week covered in the refrigerator. (I have yet to have had that happen—at my house, they're eaten within days!)

IF YOU DON'T have a wire rack for cooling the cupcakes, don't fret. Tip the cupcakes on their side to rest so that air flows freely around the bottom. That way, they won't sweat while cooling.

TO GET YOUR cupcakes a uniform size, use a cookie scoop that measures ¼ cup. This is a perfect way to get equal round tops every time.

A SMALL, UNEVEN spatula not only makes frosting cakes easier, but can also aid you in removing cupcakes from the pan. Simply slide the spatula between the paper liner and the pan, and carefully lift.

IF A RECIPE calls for butter, please do not skimp and use margarine. Not only is butter in the name, but you will be caught! Butter adds the right flavor!

DON'T RUN OUT of frosting. For 12 cupcakes you will need 1 cup frosting. For 24 cupcakes you will need 2 cups, and so on. If you plan to be more generous and pile the frosting high, add an additional cup for every 12 cupcakes.

IF YOU ARE LOOKING to trim a little fat from some recipes, you can easily substitute regular cream cheese with a reduced-fat cream cheese. But I would much rather have the real thing and less of it than more of a low-fat version.

USE DRY CAKE MIXES in the recipes unless otherwise specified.

SMALL PLASTIC sandwich bags are a perfect way to frost easily and mess-free. Scoop frosting inside the bag and squeeze all the air out. Then seal. Cut a small hole with your scissors at one bottom end of the bag. Carefully apply pressure to the bag starting at the top, aiming at the cupcake to frost. Make sure you take a test run so you are confident.

Fruity and Fabulous

Banana Cream Pie
with Whipped Cream

Banana Cream Pie

My mother-in-law makes the best banana cream pie. I have taken her twist to the ever-popular dessert and made it into a cupcake. Wow! Now this is a good cupcake!

1 box yellow cake mix

2 eggs

1 cup half-and-half

1 tsp. lemon extract

1 (4-oz.) pkg. instant banana cream pudding mix

1 recipe whipped cream

sliced bananas for garnish

MIX TOGETHER cake mix, eggs, half-and-half, lemon extract, and pudding mix (powder only).

SCOOP BATTER into paper liners, filling ¾ full.

BAKE AT 350 degrees for 15–18 minutes or until cake springs back when lightly touched. Remove from pan and allow cupcakes to cool on a wire rack.

TOP WITH whipped cream and sliced bananas to garnish.

SERVES
18-20

• • • • • • • • • • • • • • • • •

FROSTING SUGGESTIONS
Whipped Cream

Banana Foster

I found a nonalcoholic version of banana foster last summer, and my family loves it every time I make it for dessert. This over-the-top creation tastes like it takes forever to make, but in reality it takes no time at all!

1 box white cake mix

2 eggs

¼ cup butter, melted

½ cup milk

1 tsp. artificial rum flavoring

1 small jar of caramel sauce

1 recipe whipped cream

bananas for garnish

MIX TOGETHER together cake mix, eggs, butter, milk, and rum flavoring.

SCOOP BATTER into paper liners, filling ¾ full.

BAKE AT at 350 degrees for 15–18 minutes or until cake springs back when lightly touched. Remove from oven and allow to cool slightly.

SERVES
18-20

UNWRAP CUPCAKES carefully (they will be hot) and drizzle a generous amount of caramel sauce over the tops. Place a dollop of whipped cream and sliced bananas on top of the caramel sauce to garnish.

• • • • • • • • • • • • • • • • • • • •

FROSTING SUGGESTIONS
Whipped Cream

Pear Upside Down

Pears are in season at fall time. This cupcake takes advantage of fruit when it is harvested.
Canned pears work well too.

1 box white cake mix

2 eggs

½ cup oil

1 tsp. vanilla extract

¾ cup brown sugar

18–24 pear quarters, peeled

MIX TOGETHER cake mix, eggs, oil, and vanilla. Set aside. Crumble brown sugar in the bottom of the paper liners.

TOP THE sugar with 1–2 pear quarters. Pour batter on the top of the pears, and fill ¾ full.

BAKE AT 350 degrees for 15–18 minutes. Immediately turn cupcakes upside down on a serving platter. Carefully remove paper liners—they will be hot!

SERVE WITH a scoop of ice cream.

SERVES
18-20

Key Lime Pie
with Whipped Cream

Key Lime Pie

Key lime pie is the first official dessert my daughter Addie ever tasted. Her Pappy fed it to her without me knowing. At first, her mouth puckered and her eyes watered, but then she asked for more!

1 box white cake mix

3 eggs

1 cup half-and-half

6 Tbsp. key lime juice

1 can sweetened condensed milk

1 recipe whipped cream

4 Tbsp. grated lime peel (about 3 limes) for garnish

MIX TOGETHER cake mix, eggs, half-and-half, and 3 tablespoons key lime juice. Pour 1–2 tablespoons batter into each paper liner. In a separate bowl, mix sweetened condensed milk and the rest of the lime juice. Evenly divide lime milk into batter-filled cups. Top with remaining batter and fill ¾ full.

BAKE AT 350 degrees for 15–18 minutes or until cake springs back when touched lightly. Remove from oven and cool completely on a wire rack.

FROST WITH whipped cream and garnish with grated lime peel.

SERVES
18-20

• • • • • • • • • • • • • • • • • • •

FROSTING SUGGESTIONS
Whipped Cream

Lemon Blueberry

These two flavors complement each other so well. This cupcake has such a fresh taste and is so tasty for spring and summer. You can also substitute frozen berries for fresh.

1 box lemon cake mix

1 tsp. lemon extract

3 eggs

1 cup milk

1 can blueberry pie filling

powdered sugar to garnish

1 recipe whipped cream

MIX TOGETHER cake mix, lemon extract, eggs, and milk. Beat at medium speed until light and fluffy.

SCOOP 2 tablespoons cake batter into each paper liner. Add 2 tablespoons pie filling on top. Add remaining cake batter, dividing evenly among all the cupcakes.

BAKE AT 350 degrees for 15–18 minutes or until tops are light golden brown. Remove from oven and cool on a wire rack.

DUST WITH with powdered sugar and top with remaining pie filling and whipped cream.

SERVES
18-20

• • • • • • • • • • • • • • • • •

FROSTING SUGGESTIONS
Whipped Cream

Orange Creamsicle

On a hot summer day, nothing tastes better than a cold creamsicle. This cupcake, especially when served cold, is a perfect treat!

1 box yellow cake mix

2 eggs

1 cup milk

2–3 drops yellow food coloring

1–2 drops red food coloring

⅓ cup orange juice concentrate

1 recipe whipped cream

MIX TOGETHER cake mix, eggs, and milk. Drop enough yellow and red food coloring to make a good orange-colored batter. Scoop batter into paper liners and fill ¾ full.

BAKE AT 350 degrees for 15–18 minutes or until cake springs back when lightly touched. Remove from oven and place on a wire rack until cooled.

ONCE THE cupcakes are cool, cut out the top, set aside, and make a place for the filling, leaving the walls and bottom of the cupcake strong enough to support the filling.

IN A separate bowl, fold ⅓ cup orange juice concentrate into whipped cream. Spoon the filling into the hole and top with set aside portion of cupcake to seal the filling. Top with desired frosting or a dollop of any leftover filling mixture.

SERVES
18-20

FROSTING SUGGESTIONS
Cream Cheese • Vanilla Buttercream • Whipped Cream

Orange Poppy Seed
with Cream Cheese Frosting

Orange Poppy Seed

Citrus and poppy seeds give this cake a crisp, fruity, and sweet taste—perfect for your next brunch or special breakfast.

1 box yellow cake mix

2 Tbsp. poppy seeds

1 medium orange, juiced

2 Tbsp. orange zest

½ tsp. orange extract

2 eggs

½ cup milk

MIX ALL ingredients together in a large bowl.

SCOOP BATTER into paper liners, filling ¾ full.

BAKE AT 350 degrees for 15–18 minutes. Remove and allow to cool completely on a wire rack.

SERVES
18-20

FROSTING SUGGESTIONS
Cream Cheese Frosting with ½ teaspoon orange extract

Lemon Cream
with Whipped Cream

Lemon Cream

The smell of lemons refreshes you and can brighten any gloomy day. The taste is even better!

1 box lemon cake mix

2 eggs

1 cup sour cream

1 (8-oz.) pkg. cream cheese, softened

2 Tbsp. grated lemon zest

1 recipe whipped cream

1 tsp. lemon extract

½ cup crushed lemon drop candy

MIX TOGETHER cake mix, eggs, sour cream, and cream cheese until smooth and creamy. Add grated lemon zest and combine.

SCOOP BATTER into paper liners, filling ¾ full.

BAKE AT 350 degrees for 15–18 minutes or until cake springs back when lightly touched. Remove and cool cupcakes on a wire rack.

ADD LEMON extract to whipped cream and combine well. Top cooled cupcakes with lemon whipped cream and sprinkle with crushed lemon candy for garnish. (Optional: Stuff cooled cupcakes before frosting with Lemon Whipped Cream, as pictured.)

SERVES
18-20

● ● ● ● ● ● ● ● ● ● ● ● ● ● ● ● ● ● ●

FROSTING SUGGESTIONS
Lemon Whipped Cream

Peach Cobbler

There is a favorite peach cobbler recipe in my family. Here is a very easy version in a single serving cupcake form.

1 box yellow cake mix

3 eggs

½ cup butter, melted

½ cup milk

1 tsp. vanilla extract

1 tsp. cinnamon

1 tsp. nutmeg

1 pound sliced peaches (canned or fresh), peeled and drained

2 Tbsp. sugar

MIX TOGETHER cake mix, eggs, butter, milk, vanilla, cinnamon, and nutmeg.

PLACE SLICED sliced peaches in a large bowl and sprinkle sugar on top. Toss gently and set aside.

SERVES
18-20

SCOOP ABOUT 2 tablespoons batter in the bottom of each paper liner. Place equal amount of peaches on top of each batter-filled paper liner. Fill the remaining paper liner ¾ full.

BAKE AT 350 degrees for 18–20 minutes or until cake springs back when lightly touched.

SERVE WARM with ice cream or whipped cream.

Banana Streusel

My aunt made a banana cake for my mom and dad during a visit to California. I heard only raves about how delicious and moist it was. Serving this cake is now a tradition among my immediate family members. When I told my mom about this idea for an easy cupcake cookbook, she said I would have to include this recipe, only slightly modified for cupcakes.

1 box yellow cake mix, ½ cup reserved for topping

3 eggs

1 cup half-and-half

1 tsp. vanilla extract

4 Tbsp. butter, melted

3 ripe bananas, peeled and mashed

3 Tbsp. butter

½ tsp. cinnamon

sliced bananas for garnish

MIX TOGETHER cake mix, eggs, half-and-half, vanilla, and melted butter until smooth. Fold mashed bananas into batter, and fill the paper liners ¾ full.

POUR BATTER into a small bowl and add ½ cup dry cake mix, butter, and cinnamon. Combine with a fork to make crumbs. Evenly sprinkle the crumb mixture on top of all the unbaked cupcakes.

SERVES
18-20

BAKE AT at 350 degrees for 15–18 minutes or until slightly golden brown. Do not overbake—this causes a dry cupcake. Remove from oven and allow to cool slightly before serving with ice cream on the side, or cool completely on a wire rack and frost.

TOP WITH whipped cream and sliced bananas to garnish.

• •
FROSTING SUGGESTIONS
Vanilla Buttercream • Cream Cheese • Whipped Cream

Orange Cranberry
Upside Down

Orange Cranberry Upside Down

When I think of fall time, I think of all the great food that is associated with the season. Apples, spices, cranberries, and oranges. Here is a great cupcake with all the flavors of fall in each bite.

BONUS RECIPE!

1 box yellow cake mix

1 large orange, zested and juiced (zest first, then juice)

3 eggs

½ cup whole milk

1 can whole cranberry sauce

MIX TOGETHER cake mix, orange zest and juice, eggs, and milk. Set aside.

STIR THE cranberry sauce until well combined and place 1 tablespoon in the bottom of each paper liner. Scoop the cake batter into the paper liner, filling ¾ full.

BAKE AT 350 degrees for 15–18 minutes until cake springs back when lightly touched. Remove cupcakes from the oven and cool slightly. Carefully remove the cupcake liner (it will be hot) and turn cupcake upside down on a platter.

TOP WITH powdered sugar or serve with a scoop of your favorite vanilla ice cream if desired. You can even sprinkle with cinnamon too.

SERVES 18-20

• •

FROSTING SUGGESTIONS
Whipped Cream

Pineapple
Upside Down

Pineapple Upside Down

This cupcake is best when served warm (upside down) with a scoop of ice cream.
An easy dessert for a summer luau or any special occasion.

1 box yellow cake mix

3 eggs

pineapple juice from crushed pineapple (see below), plus milk to equal 1 cup

¾ cup brown sugar

1 can (½ cup) crushed pineapple, drained with juice reserved

1 recipe whipped cream

maraschino cherries for garnish

MIX TOGETHER cake mix, eggs, and pineapple juice plus milk to equal 1 cup. Beat until smooth.

DIVIDE BROWN sugar among all paper liners equally. Place pineapple chunks in paper liner. Top with cake batter and fill ¾ full.

BAKE AT 350 degrees for 15–18 minutes or until cake springs back when lightly touched. Immediately flip each cupcake over onto a large platter and remove paper liner carefully—they will be hot!

SERVE WITH whipped cream and garnish with a cherry.

SERVES
18-20

FROSTING SUGGESTIONS
Whipped Cream

Tutti Frutti

This cupcake is a take on the ever-so-popular holiday treat. But my version is the best yet!

1 box yellow cake mix

3 eggs

¼ cup oil

1 tsp. vanilla extract

1 can fruit cocktail with juice

MIX TOGETHER all ingredients.

SCOOP BATTER into paper liners, filling ¾ full.

BAKE AT 350 degrees for 15–18 minutes until cake springs back when lightly touched. Remove from oven and cool on a wire rack.

SERVE WITH a scoop of ice cream or whipped cream.

SERVES
18-20

Vanilla Pudding Poppy Seed

This is a great cupcake for a brunch or a late afternoon snack. You can enjoy the softness of the sweet cupcake with or without frosting.

1 box yellow cake mix

1 (4-oz.) pkg. vanilla pudding mix (powder only)

2 Tbsp. poppy seeds

3 eggs

1 cup milk

1 tsp. vanilla extract

MIX TOGETHER all ingredients.

SCOOP BATTER into paper liners, filling ¾ full.

BAKE AT 350 degrees for 15–18 minutes or until cake springs back when lightly touched. Remove from the oven and cool on a wire rack.

SERVES
18-20

• • • • • • • • • • • • • • • • • •

FROSTING SUGGESTIONS
Vanilla Buttercream

Sour Cream Blueberry
with Whipped Cream

Sour Cream Blueberry

This cupcake has an eye-catching presentation. It is truly picture perfect.

1 box yellow cake mix

2 eggs

1 cup sour cream

1 tsp. vanilla extract

powdered sugar to garnish

1 recipe whipped cream

1 cup fresh or frozen blueberries

MIX TOGETHER cake mix, eggs, sour cream, and vanilla.

SCOOP BATTER into paper liners, filling ¾ full.

BAKE AT 350 degrees for 15–18 minutes. Cupcake tops will not be rounded.

REMOVE FROM pan and allow to cool completely on a wire rack.

DUST TOP with powdered sugar and serve with a dollop of whipped cream and blueberries to garnish.

SERVES
18-20

• • • • • • • • • • • • • • • • •

FROSTING SUGGESTIONS
Whipped Cream

Piña Colada
with Whipped Cream

Piña Colada

Light and refreshing, these cupcakes will truly satisfy your sweet tooth. They're almost as good as the real thing.

1 box yellow cake mix

3 eggs

1 tsp. coconut extract

½ cup buttermilk

1 small can crushed pineapple

1 recipe whipped cream

MIX TOGETHER cake mix, eggs, coconut extract, buttermilk, and pineapple with juice.

SCOOP BATTER into paper liners, filling ¾ full.

BAKE AT 350 degrees for 15–18 minutes or until cake springs back when lightly touched. Remove from pan and allow to cool on a wire rack.

SERVES
18-20

• • • • • • • • • • • • • • • • • •

FROSTING SUGGESTIONS
Whipped Cream

Pink Lemonade

This is a perfect treat for summertime. What if you made a batch for your kids to sell at their next lemonade stand? They wouldn't last very long!

1 box white cake mix

⅓ cup pink lemonade concentrate

½ cup buttermilk

3 eggs

2–3 drops red food coloring

MIX TOGETHER all ingredients until smooth.

SCOOP BATTER into paper liners, filling ¾ full.

BAKE AT 350 degrees for 15–18 minutes or until cake springs back when lightly touched.

COOL COMPLETELY before frosting.

SERVES
18-20

FROSTING SUGGESTIONS
Cream Cheese • Pink Lemonade Cream • Whipped Cream

Strawberry Cheesecake

Cheesecake, yummy cheesecake! Whenever I can choose my dessert, I pick cheesecake every time!

1 box white cake mix

3 eggs

1 cup milk

1 tsp. vanilla extract

1 cup sugar

1 (8-oz.) pkg. cream cheese, softened

2 cups whipped topping

1 cup sliced strawberries for garnish

MIX TOGETHER cake mix, eggs, milk, and vanilla.

SCOOP BATTER into paper liners, filling ¾ full.

BAKE AT 350 degrees for 15–18 minutes or until cake springs back when touched lightly. Remove from pan and allow to cool completely. Cut top portion off and set aside to make a small cavity in each cupcake.

IN A large mixing bowl, cream together sugar, cream cheese, and whipped topping. Spoon filling into each hole in the cupcake, gently replacing the top of the cake to seal.

FROST AND garnish with strawberries.

SERVES
18-20

• • • • • • • • • • • • • • • •

FROSTING SUGGESTIONS
Whipped Cream • Vanilla Buttercream

Coconut Cream Pie

Coconut Cream Pie

For Holly and Shelley. Thank you for your support and encouragement.
And for putting the idea in my head for this wonderful recipe.

BONUS RECIPE!

1 box yellow cake mix

2 tsps. coconut extract

3 eggs

1 cup half-and-half

1 cup shredded coconut

½ cup shredded coconut, toasted for garnish

MIX TOGETHER cake mix, 1 teaspoon coconut extract, eggs, and half-and-half. Add shredded coconut to batter. Fold in to combine.

SCOOP BATTER into paper liners, filling ¾ full.

BAKE AT 350 degrees for 15–18 minutes until cupcakes spring back when lightly touched. Remove from oven and cool completely.

MEANWHILE, MIX together vanilla buttercream frosting with remaining 1 teaspoon coconut extract. Frost the cooled cupcakes and top with toasted coconut for garnish.

SERVES 18-20

• • • • • • • • • • • • • • • • • • •

FROSTING SUGGESTIONS

Vanilla Buttercream Frosting with 1 teaspoon coconut extract

White Chocolate Strawberry

The name of this cupcake says it all, doesn't it?

2 cups white chocolate chips

1 box white cake mix

2 eggs

1 cup milk

1 tsp. vanilla extract

white chocolate chunks for garnish

strawberries for garnish

MELT WHITE chocolate chips in the microwave 20 seconds at a time, stirring in between, until smooth. Do not overheat chocolate (it burns easily). Set aside to cool.

MIX TOGETHER cake mix, eggs, milk, and vanilla. Fold melted white chocolate into batter and stir to combine.

SERVES 18–20

SCOOP BATTER into paper liners, filling ¾ full.

BAKE AT 350 degrees for 15–18 minutes. Remove from oven and cool completely on a wire rack.

FROST AND top with white chocolate chunks and strawberries to garnish.

• • • • • • • • • • • • • • • • • • •

FROSTING SUGGESTIONS
White Chocolate Mousse • Whipped Cream • Vanilla Buttercream

Yogurt Parfait

The yogurt in this cupcake creates a unique tang and flavor. I never thought I'd offer my children a cupcake for breakfast, but this one is really good!

1 box white cake mix

1 (6-oz.) container vanilla yogurt

½ cup milk

2 eggs

1½ cups granola

2 cups diced berries (blackberries, strawberries, etc.) for garnish

MIX TOGETHER cake mix, yogurt, milk, and eggs. Fold in ¾ cup granola.

SCOOP BATTER into paper liners, filling ¾ full. Sprinkle unbaked cupcakes with remaining granola.

BAKE AT 350 degrees for 15–18 minutes until cake springs back when lightly touched. Remove from oven and cool.

TOP WITH diced berries just before serving.

SERVES
18-20

Strawberry Shortcake
with Whipped Cream

Strawberry Shortcake

This dessert is known for its light and fresh taste. It's a summer staple for an after-dinner treat, especially when strawberries are in season.

2 cups diced strawberries

2 Tbsp. sugar

1 box white cake mix

2 eggs

1 cup whipping cream

1 tsp. vanilla extract

¼ tsp. salt

1 recipe whipped cream

ADD SUGAR to strawberries in a medium bowl. Stir and set aside. Mix together cake mix, eggs, whipping cream, vanilla, and salt.

SCOOP 1–2 tablespoons batter into paper liners. Add 2 tablespoons strawberry mixture on top. Cover strawberries with more batter and fill ¾ full. Save extra strawberries for garnish.

BAKE AT 350 degrees for 15–18 minutes or until cake springs back when lightly touched. Allow cake to cool slightly before serving with whipped cream and strawberries.

SERVES
18-20

• • • • • • • • • • • • • • • • • •

FROSTING SUGGESTIONS
Whipped Cream

Strawberry Daiquiri

Sipping nice cool strawberry daiquiris on the beach, watching the waves curl into the sand . . . paradise.

BONUS RECIPE!

1 box white cake mix

2 eggs

½ cup strawberry daiquiri mix

½ cup sour cream

½ cup half-and-half

1 recipe Whipped Cream

2 Tbsp. grated lime zest

Fresh strawberries for garnish

MIX TOGETHER cake mix, eggs, strawberry daiquiri mix, sour cream, and half-and-half. Batter will be thick.

SCOOP BATTER into paper liners, filling ¾ full.

BAKE AT 350 degrees for 15–18 minutes. Remove from the oven and cool completely.

SERVES 18-20

FROST WITH whipped cream and garnish with whole or sliced fresh strawberries and lime zest.

• • • • • • • • • • • • • • • • •

FROSTING SUGGESTIONS
Whipped Cream

Best Ever Apple

I saw the best recipe for an apple cake on a cooking program years ago. It was loaded with saturated fat and sugar, which I try not to serve my family. I reinvented this cake and made it better tasting and better for you. Now it's a cupcake too!

1 box spice cake mix

2 eggs

2 tsp. vanilla extract

1 tsp. cinnamon

½ cup oil

2 Granny Smith apples cut into ½-inch pieces, skins on

MIX TOGETHER cake mix, eggs, vanilla, cinnamon, and oil. Batter will be thick.

ADD APPLES and beat for 2–3 minutes on medium speed. Batter will thin out somewhat. Pour batter into paper liners and fill ¾ full.

BAKE AT 350 degrees for 18–20 minutes or until cake springs back when lightly touched. Remove from oven and cool completely on a wire rack. Frost once cooled.

SERVES
18-20

FROSTING SUGGESTIONS
Caramel Cream • Cream Cheese

The Sweetness of Chocolate

Double Fudge

Double Fudge

Is there really anything better than double fudge? The saying, "Hand over the chocolate and nobody gets hurt!" definitely applies to these little cakes.

1 box chocolate cake mix

3 eggs

1 cup heavy cream (or half-and-half)

1 cup semi-sweet chocolate chips, melted

1 cup semi-sweet chocolate chips

MIX TOGETHER cake mix, eggs, and cream. Fold in melted chocolate chips and regular chocolate chips.

SCOOP BATTER into paper liners, filling ¾ full.

BAKE AT 350 degrees for 15–18 minutes or until cupcakes spring back when lightly touched. Place on a rack and cool completely.

FROST WHEN cooled.

SERVES
18-20

• • • • • • • • • • • • • • • • • • • •

FROSTING SUGGESTIONS
Chocolate Buttercream • Chocolate Ganache

Burnt Almond Fudge

Is your mouth watering after reading this cupcake title? Can you taste the roasted almonds and rich, creamy fudge? Why not make this cupcake for dessert tonight?

1 box dark chocolate cake mix

2 eggs

1 cup half-and-half

1 tsp. almond extract

2 cups chocolate chunks or chocolate chips

1 cup slivered almonds, roasted

MIX TOGETHER cake mix, eggs, half-and-half, and extract. Fold chocolate chunks and roasted almonds into batter.

SCOOP BATTER into paper liners, filling ¾ full.

BAKE AT 350 degrees for 15–18 minutes or until cake springs back when lightly touched. Remove from oven and cool on a wire rack.

SERVES
18-20

FROSTING SUGGESTIONS
Chocolate Ganache • Chocolate Buttercream

Chocolate Almond

Almond is a perfect pairing with chocolate.

1 box chocolate cake mix

1 tsp. almond extract

1 cup chocolate chips

3 eggs

1 cup milk

1 cup slivered almonds for garnish

MIX TOGETHER all ingredients except slivered almonds.

SCOOP BATTER into paper liners, filling ¾ full.

BAKE AT 350 degrees for 15–18 minutes or until top of cupcake springs back when lightly touched. Remove from oven and cool completely on a rack.

FROST COOLED cupcakes and top with slivered almonds.

SERVES
18-20

FROSTING SUGGESTIONS
Chocolate Buttercream • Chocolate Mousse

Chocolate Cream
with Chocolate Ganache

Chocolate Cream

Chocolate cream cupcakes are simple to prepare yet elegant and full of rich chocolate flavors.

I box chocolate cake mix

3 eggs

I cup sour cream

2 cups heavy whipping cream

¼ cup powdered sugar

½ cup grated chocolate for garnish

MIX TOGETHER cake mix, eggs, and sour cream until smooth.

POUR BATTER into paper liners and fill ¾ full.

BAKE AT 350 degrees for 15–18 minutes or until cake springs back when lightly touched.

COOL COMPLETELY on a wire rack. When cooled, cut the top off and pull out some of the cake, leaving a solid wall of cake to support the filling. Whip the cream until stiff peaks form and add powdered sugar. Add whipped cream by the spoonful to the holes of all cupcakes and top with cupcake lid.

FROST WITH desired frosting and garnish with grated chocolate.

SERVES
18-20

FROSTING SUGGESTIONS

Whipped Cream • Chocolate Buttercream • Chocolate Ganache

Black Forest
with Chocolate Ganache

Black Forest

As a child, I watched my grandpa eat chocolate-covered cherries as a special treat. Many years later, we discovered he only ate them because we gave them to him as a present. He truly didn't like them at all! But I sure enjoyed them.

1 box chocolate cake mix

3 eggs

½ cup sour cream

1 tsp. almond extract

1 large can cherry pie filling, reserving 1 cup for topping

MIX TOGETHER cake mix, eggs, sour cream, almond extract, and pie filling until cake mix is moist. Do not overmix.

POUR BATTER into paper liners and fill ¾ full.

BAKE AT 350 degrees for 17–19 minutes or until barely done in center. Remove from oven and allow to cool completely on a rack.

FROST CUPCAKES, making a slight edge around the cupcake to hold the cherry filling.

ADD 1 tablespoon filling to the top of each cupcake.

SERVES
18-20

FROSTING SUGGESTIONS
Chocolate Buttercream • Chocolate Ganache

Chocolate Chip Oatmeal

Chocolate chips in oatmeal cake with numerous possibilities for frosting. You can take this cupcake and make it all your own.

1 box chocolate cake mix

2 eggs

1 cup quick oats

½ cup milk

¼ cup oil

1 tsp. vanilla extract

1 cup chocolate chips

MIX TOGETHER all ingredients until batter is moistened.

SCOOP BATTER into paper liners, filling ¾ full.

BAKE AT 350 degrees for 15–18 minutes or until cake springs back when lightly touched. Remove from the oven and cool completely.

SERVES
18-20

• • • • • • • • • • • • • • • • •

FROSTING SUGGESTIONS
Chocolate Ganache • Chocolate Buttercream • Chocolate Sour Cream •
Vanilla Buttercream

Chocolate Chip Zucchini

I'm always looking for ways to use zucchini from my garden. My kids beg me to make this recipe. I don't mind making this sweet treat because it is full of vegetables! It also freezes well, without the frosting.

1 box chocolate cake mix

3 eggs

½ cup oil

1 cup grated zucchini

1 tsp. vanilla extract

1 cup chocolate chips

MIX TOGETHER all ingredients until well combined.

SCOOP BATTER into paper liners, filling ¾ full.

BAKE AT 350 degrees for 15–18 minutes or until cake springs back when lightly touched. Cool completely on a wire rack.

SERVES
18-20

• • • • • • • • • • • • • • • • • •

FROSTING SUGGESTIONS

Chocolate Buttercream • Chocolate Ganache

Cookie Dough
with Whipped Cream

Cookie Dough

The sweetness of cookie dough and a light, fluffy cupcake together is awesome. Mini cupcakes are a great after-school treat and a hit on a tray at a party.

1 box chocolate cake mix

3 eggs

1 tsp. vanilla extract

1 cup milk

1 pkg. ready-made chocolate chip cookie dough

1 recipe whipped cream

1 cup mini chocolate chips for garnish

MIX TOGETHER cake mix, eggs, vanilla, and milk.

DROP 1 tablespoon of batter into the paper liners, filling all 24. Add 1 tablespoon of rounded cookie dough on top of the batter in each liner. Scoop the remaining batter on top of the cookie dough until all liners are ¾ full.

BAKE AT 350 degrees for 15–18 minutes or until cake springs back when lightly touched. Remove and cool on a wire rack.

FROST COOLED cupcakes with whipped cream and mini chocolate chips.

SERVES
24

FROSTING SUGGESTIONS
Whipped Cream

Cookies and
Cream Dream
with Vanilla Buttercream

Cookies and Cream Dream

Cookies and cream make anything taste great! These cupcakes go so fast after they're baked—
be sure to hide a few for yourself.

1 box chocolate cake mix

1 cup sour cream

3 eggs

1 tsp. vanilla extract

18–24 whole chocolate sandwich cookies

12 chocolate sandwich cookies, crumbled

MIX TOGETHER cake mix, sour cream, eggs, and vanilla. Place a spoonful of batter on the bottom of each paper liner. Place a whole cookie on the bottom lying flat. Cover with remaining batter until ¾ full.

BAKE AT 350 degrees for 15–18 minutes. Allow cupcakes to cool completely on a rack.

ADD CRUMBLED cookies to buttercream frosting. Be generous and frost cupcakes nice and high.

SERVES
18-20

FROSTING SUGGESTIONS
Vanilla Buttercream

Chocolate Angels

These chocolate cupcakes are light and airy—a delicious dessert or treat anytime.

1 angel food cake mix

⅓ cup cocoa

1¼ cups water

1 recipe whipped cream

strawberries (fresh or frozen) for garnish

MIX TOGETHER cake mix and cocoa in a glass or metal bowl and whisk until combined. Add water and beat on low speed until moistened. Mix on medium speed for 1 minute.

SCOOP BATTER into paper liners, filling ⅔ full.

BAKE AT 350 degrees for 20–30 minutes or until light golden brown. Immediately remove from pan and cool on a wire rack.

SERVE WITH a dollop of whipped cream and strawberries.

SERVES
18-20

FROSTING SUGGESTIONS
Whipped Cream • Chocolate Mousse • White Chocolate Mousse

Chocolate Chip Mint

One of my favorite ice cream flavors is chocolate chip mint. Why not make a cupcake with the same great taste? Mint and chocolate are the perfect combination.

3 eggs

1 cup milk

1 box chocolate cake mix

1 tsp. mint extract

1¼ cups mini chocolate chips (semi-sweet is best)

IN A medium mixing bowl, whisk eggs until fluffy. Add milk and stir. Pour dry cake mix into egg mixture and stir until combined. Do not overstir. Add mint extract and 1 cup of the mini chocolate chips.

SCOOP BATTER into paper liners, filling ¾ full.

BAKE AT 350 degrees for 15–18 minutes or until cake springs back when lightly touched with your finger. Remove from pan and place cupcakes on a rack to cool.

FROST WITH desired frosting and sprinkle remaining chocolate chips on top.

SERVES
18-20

• • • • • • • • • • • • • • • • • • •

FROSTING SUGGESTIONS

White Chocolate Mint • Chocolate Buttercream

Chocolate Peanut
Butter Crumble

Chocolate Peanut Butter Crumble

I love the taste of chocolate and peanut butter together—chocolate and peanut butter cookies, peanut butter with chocolate syrup on ice cream, a spoonful of peanut butter with some chocolate chips sprinkled on top! Is your mouth watering like mine is now? This is my favorite cupcake. I hope it will become one of yours too!

1 box chocolate cake mix, ½ cup reserved

3 eggs

1 cup milk

2 cups peanut butter chips

½ cup quick oats

4 Tbsp. butter, softened

ice cream

chocolate syrup

MIX TOGETHER cake mix, eggs, and milk. In a separate bowl, place peanut butter chips, oats, butter, and remaining ½ cup reserved cake mix. Mix together with a fork until small crumbles appear.

SCOOP BATTER into paper liners, filling ⅔ full. Top with a spoonful of peanut butter crumbles, dividing evenly among all cupcakes.

BAKE AT 350 degrees for 18–20 minutes. Cake will be uneven on top.

SERVE WITH garnish of ice cream on the top of these warm cupcakes, drizzled with chocolate syrup.

SERVES
18-20

Hot Chocolate

This recipe was inspired from a cold, snowy, wintry day… After shoveling what felt like four feet of snow, we made hot chocolate, and I thought, "A hot chocolate cupcake would be fantastic."

BONUS RECIPE!

1 box dark chocolate or chocolate fudge cake mix
3 eggs
1 tsp. vanilla extract
1 cup milk or half-and-half
Mini marshmallows

MIX TOGETHER cake mix, eggs, vanilla extract, and milk.

SCOOP BATTER into paper liners, filling ¾ full.

BAKE AT 350 degrees for 15–18 minutes. Remove from oven and cool completely.

FROST COOLED cupcakes with frosting or whipped cream and top with marshmallows.

SERVES
18-20

FROSTING SUGGESTIONS
Vanilla Buttercream • Whipped Cream

Chocolate Caramel Surprise

For all you caramel lovers, this is your cupcake of choice! Serve these little cakes with frosting or a little warm with a dusting of powdered sugar and whipped cream on the side.

1 box chocolate cake mix

2 eggs

½ cup milk

½ cup oil

1 tsp. vanilla extract

1 pkg. chocolate-covered caramels

MIX TOGETHER cake mix, eggs, milk, oil, and vanilla until light and fluffy.

LINE CUPCAKE pan with paper liners. Layer a spoonful of cake batter. Add 1–2 chocolate caramels on top of the batter.

SCOOP BATTER into paper liners, filling ¾ full.

BAKE AT 350 degrees for 15–18 minutes or until cake springs back when lightly touched.

SERVES
18-20

• • • • • • • • • • • • • • • • •

FROSTING SUGGESTIONS
Caramel Cream • Chocolate Buttercream • Chocolate Ganache

Chocolate
Peanut Butter Cup
with Chocolate Buttercream

Chocolate Peanut Butter Cup

My neighbor said these cupcakes are sinful. But believe me, they are worth every bite.

1 box chocolate cake mix

3 eggs

1 cup milk

1 bag chocolate peanut butter cups

MIX TOGETHER cake mix, eggs, and milk.

SCOOP 2 tablespoons batter into paper liners and place a peanut butter cup on top. Fill paper liners ¾ full with remaining batter.

BAKE AT 350 degrees for 15–18 minutes or until the cake springs back when lightly touched. Remove from oven and allow to cool on a wire rack. When completely cooled, frost.

SERVES
18-20

FROSTING SUGGESTIONS
Peanut Butter • Chocolate Buttercream

German Chocolate

German Chocolate

For my sweet sister-in-law Amber. She loves a good German chocolate cake.
Better yet, a German chocolate cupcake.

1 box German chocolate cake mix

3 eggs

1 cup milk

1 tsp. vanilla extract

¾ cup mini semi-sweet chocolate chips

2 cups toasted coconut

Caramel ice cream topping

MIX TOGETHER cake mix, eggs, milk, vanilla, and chocolate chips. Batter will be thick.

SCOOP BATTER into paper liners, filling ¾ full.

BAKE AT 350 degrees for 15–18 minutes. Remove cupcakes and cool completely.

FROST WITH chocolate frosting and top with coconut. Drizzle with caramel ice cream topping.

SERVES
18-20

FROSTING SUGGESTIONS
Chocolate Buttercream Frosting

Chocolate Cinnamon

Surprisingly, chocolate and cinnamon taste great together. And cinnamon has been proven to be good for you. So eat one, and don't feel too guilty!

1 box dark chocolate cake mix

2 eggs

1 cup milk

1 tsp. vanilla extract

2 Tbsp. cinnamon

MIX TOGETHER all ingredients.

POUR BATTER into paper liners and fill ¾ full.

BAKE AT 350 degrees for 15–18 minutes or until cake springs back when lightly touched. Remove from oven and cool completely.

SERVES
18-20

· · · · · · · · · · · · · · · · ·

FROSTING SUGGESTIONS
Chocolate Ganache   •   Chocolate Buttercream

Chocolate Mayonnaise

My mom makes this cake for special family parties, and we usually have it for a birthday celebration. What makes this cake even more special is the cream cheese frosting. Trust me on this one!

I box chocolate cake mix

I cup mayonnaise (you can use reduced fat)

¼ cup water

I tsp. vanilla extract

MIX TOGETHER all ingredients.

SCOOP BATTER into paper liners, filling ¾ full.

BAKE AT 350 degrees for 15–18 minutes or until cake springs back when lightly touched. Remove and cool on a wire rack.

FROST WITH cream cheese frosting.

SERVES
18-20

• • • • • • • • • • • • • • • • • • •

FROSTING SUGGESTIONS
Cream Cheese

Chocolate Raspberry
Trifle with Whipped Cream

Chocolate Raspberry Trifle

Some of my friends ask me to make a chocolate raspberry trifle when we go to their home for dinner and dessert. Here is a smaller version, cupcake style.

1 chocolate cake mix

1 (4-oz.) pkg. chocolate pudding powder

2 eggs

½ cup milk

1 recipe chocolate ganache

1 cup raspberries for garnish

MIX TOGETHER cake mix, pudding powder, eggs, and milk. **and water, and oil.**

SCOOP BATTER into paper liners, filling ¾ full.

BAKE AT 350 degrees for 15–18 minutes or until cake springs back when lightly touched. Remove from the oven and cool on a wire rack.

TOP WITH chocolate ganache frosting and top with raspberries.

SERVES
18-20

FROSTING SUGGESTIONS

Chocolate Ganache • Chocolate Buttercream • Whipped Cream
Peanut Butter • Cream Cheese

Melting Surprise
with Whipped Cream

Melting Surprise

This is a take on chocolate molten cake. But there is just something about unwrapping this little cupcake that is so much fun!

1 box chocolate cake mix

4 eggs

1 tsp. vanilla extract

½ cup sour cream

1 (8-oz.) pkg. cream cheese, softened

½ cup sugar

1 cup semi-sweet chocolate chips, melted

MIX TOGETHER cake mix, 3 eggs, vanilla, and sour cream. Set aside.

IN A separate bowl, add softened cream cheese, 1 egg, sugar, and melted chocolate chips. Stir until combined well.

SCOOP BATTER into paper liners, filling ¾ full. Add 1 teaspoon filling to the top of each cupcake.

BAKE AT 350 degrees for 20 minutes, being careful not to overbake.

TOP WITH whipped cream and grated chocolate.

SERVES
18-20

• • • • • • • • • • • • • • • • • •

FROSTING SUGGESTIONS
Whipped Cream

It's a Rocky Road

Your cake and ice cream should go hand in hand, right? Why not mix this one up a bit too?

1 box chocolate cake mix

3 eggs

1 cup milk

1 cup chopped walnuts

1 cup chocolate chips

1–2 cups mini marshmallows

MIX TOGETHER cake mix, eggs, and milk.

SCOOP BATTER into paper liners, filling ¾ full.

BAKE AT 350 degrees for 12 minutes. Remove from oven. Quickly place walnuts, chocolate chips, and marshmallows on the center of each cupcake, dividing evenly.

RETURN TO oven for 3–4 more minutes. Marshmallows will turn golden. Remove from oven and cool completely on a wire rack. Serve while still warm if desired.

SERVES
18-20

Little Earthquake

This cupcake gets its name from the way it looks—a little shaky in the beginning, and a whole lot rocky (nutty) in the end.

1 box German chocolate cake mix

3 eggs

1 cup milk

1 cup shredded coconut

1 cup chopped pecans

4 Tbsp. butter, melted

½ (4-oz.) pkg. cream cheese, softened

2 cups powdered sugar

MIX TOGETHER cake mix, eggs, and milk. In a separate bowl, combine coconut and pecans. Divide and scatter nut mixture evenly in the bottom of each paper cupcake liner and set aside.

CREAM MELTED butter, cream cheese, and powdered sugar in a large bowl. Beat until light and smooth. Set aside.

SCOOP CHOCOLATE batter on top of nut mixture, filling each paper liner ⅔ full. Place a spoonful of cream cheese mixture on top of the cupcake.

BAKE AT 350 degrees for 15–18 minutes. The topping will seem a little wobbly, but the cupcake will set as it cools. Remove cupcakes from oven and place on a rack until completely cool.

DUST WITH powdered sugar before serving.

SERVES
18-20

Give Me S'more

Give Me S'more

S'mores are an essential part of camping. This cupcake brings part of the camping experience to your home anytime. If you want a bite-size treat, make these cupcakes with mini paper liners. Cut the graham crackers with a serrated knife for a custom fit.

I box white cake mix

2 eggs

I cup milk

I bag large marshmallows

I jar chocolate fudge sauce

graham crackers (broken into squares)

MIX TOGETHER cake mix, eggs, and milk.

SCOOP BATTER into paper liners, filling ¾ full. Place one large marshmallow in the center of the unbaked cupcake and press down slightly to submerge marshmallow.

BAKE AT 350 degrees for 15–18 minutes or until marshmallow is golden and cake springs back when lightly touched. Remove from oven and cool on a wire rack.

WARM FUDGE sauce in the microwave and place a spoonful on top of each cupcake. Top with a graham cracker square.

SERVES 18-20

• • • • • • • • • • • • • • • • • • •

FROSTING SUGGESTIONS
Whipped Cream

Mint Patty Brownie

These brownie cupcakes will be gone before they have cooled on your rack. Your family will smell them from a mile away!

1 dark chocolate brownie mix (family size)

2 eggs

¼ cup water

1 tsp. vanilla extract

⅓ cup oil

1 bag mint patties

MIX TOGETHER brownie mix, eggs, water, vanilla, and oil. Stir until moistened.

POUR ABOUT 2 tablespoons batter in every paper liner. Layer 2 mint patties in each liner. Top with remaining batter, filling ¾ full.

BAKE AT 350 degrees for 13–15 minutes until soft but not too wiggly. The middle will be gooey and delicious.

COOL COMPLETELY on a wire rack. Dust with powdered sugar or frost.

SERVES
18-20

• • • • • • • • • • • • • • • • • •

FROSTING SUGGESTIONS
Chocolate Buttercream • Chocolate Ganache • Chocolate Mousse • Whipped Cre

Oreo Cookie

My children have a favorite treat at Grandma's house—Oreos and milk. Here's a cupcake with my children in mind. Those chocolate smiles warm my heart every time!

1 box chocolate cake mix

3 eggs

1 cup milk

18–20 Oreo cookies

MIX TOGETHER cake mix, eggs, and milk.

SCOOP BATTER into paper liners, filling ½ full. Place a whole Oreo cookie on top and push down slightly to submerge. Cover with remaining batter and fill ¾ full.

BAKE AT 350 degrees for 15–18 minutes or until cake springs back when lightly touched. Remove from the oven and cool completely before frosting.

SERVES
18-20

FROSTING SUGGESTIONS
Chocolate Ganache   •   Chocolate Buttercream

Nanaimo Brownie

Nanaimo Brownie

Several years ago on a trip with my husband, I came across a phenomenal treat in British Columbia called nanaimo bars. I have taken this brownie cupcake and added the traditional ingredients to make it shine. Holy cow!

1 box dark chocolate brownie mix (family size)

2 eggs

⅓ cup oil

½ cup water

1 cup shredded coconut

1 cup chopped almonds

2 cups heavy whipping cream

4 Tbsp. Bird's custard powder

⅓ cup powdered sugar

2 Tbsp. butter

4 Tbsp. semi-sweet chocolate chips

MIX TOGETHER brownie mix, eggs, oil, and water. Stir until moistened. In a separate bowl, combine coconut and chopped almonds. Spoon nut mixture evenly into paper liners.

POUR BATTER into paper liners and fill ¾ full.

BAKE AT 350 degrees for 13–15 minutes until soft in the center. Remove and cool completely on a wire rack.

SERVES
18–20

MEANWHILE, WHIP the cream until firm peaks form. Add custard powder and powdered sugar and combine well. Frost cooled cupcakes with the custard—be generous!

MELT BUTTER and chocolate in a small bowl in the microwave. Be careful not to burn the chocolate. Stir every 20 seconds. Drizzle cooled chocolate over the custard cream topping.

Slippery Butterfingers

My husband came up with this idea—crushed candy bars baked into the actual cupcake to add texture and dimension to every bite. It's delicious!

1 box yellow cake mix

3 eggs

¼ cup oil

½ cup milk

1 tsp. vanilla extract

2 cups crushed Butterfinger candy bar

MIX TOGETHER cake mix, eggs, oil, milk, and vanilla. Add 1 cup crushed candy to batter.

POUR BATTER into paper liners and fill ¾ full.

BAKE AT 350 degrees for 15–18 minutes or until cake springs back when lightly touched. Remove from oven and cool completely.

COOL AND top with remaining crushed candy.

SERVES
18-20

FROSTING SUGGESTIONS
Chocolate Buttercream • Vanilla Buttercream

Sour Cream Chocolate

Sour cream is so good in both the cake and the frosting. Make this cupcake and pair it with chocolate sour cream frosting or whichever frosting pleases your taste.

1 box dark chocolate cake mix

2 eggs

½ cup vegetable oil

1 cup sour cream

1 tsp. vanilla extract

MIX TOGETHER cake mix, eggs, vegetable oil, sour cream, and vanilla.

POUR BATTER into paper liners and fill ¾ full.

BAKE AT 350 degrees for 15–18 minutes or until cake springs back when lightly touched. Remove from oven and cool completely before frosting.

SERVES
18-20

• • • • • • • • • • • • • • • •

FROSTING SUGGESTIONS
Chocolate Sour Cream • Chocolate Buttercream

White Chocolate
Vanilla

White Chocolate Vanilla

Even though white chocolate technically isn't chocolate, it pairs so well with vanilla. When you place a generous layer of frosting and chunks of white chocolate on top as a garnish, it's like a dream come true.

1 box white cake mix

1 cup white chocolate chips

1 tsp. vanilla extract

1 cup milk

2 eggs

½ cup oil

1 cup white chocolate chunks

MIX TOGETHER cake mix, white chocolate chips, vanilla, milk, eggs, and oil.

SCOOP BATTER into paper liners, filling ¾ full.

BAKE AT 350 degrees for 15–18 minutes or until cake springs back when lightly touched. Allow to cool completely on wire rack.

FROST WITH white chocolate frosting and garnish with white chocolate chunks.

SERVES
18-20

• • • • • • • • • • • • • • • •

FROSTING SUGGESTIONS
White Chocolate

Chocolate Fudge Brownie

A good brownie can make a hungry person happy. Here's a dark chocolate brownie that takes the cake!

1 dark chocolate brownie mix (family size)

¼ cup water

⅓ cup oil

2 eggs

1 tsp. almond extract

2 cups semi-sweet chocolate chunks

MIX TOGETHER all ingredients.

SCOOP BATTER into paper liners, filling ¾ full.

BAKE AT 350 degrees for 13–15 minutes until soft but not too wiggly. The middle will be gooey and delicious.

SERVE WARM with ice cream or frost after completely cooling on a wire rack.

SERVES
18-20

FROSTING SUGGESTIONS
Chocolate Ganache • Chocolate Buttercream • Peanut Butter • Cream Cheese

Holiday Treats

Angel Food
Toasted Coconut
with Vanilla Buttercream

Angel Food Toasted Coconut

This cupcake is so beautiful, you almost don't want to eat it. The toasted coconut on top is eye-catching and gives a crunchy and chewy texture to the cake.

1 box angel food cake mix

1 ¼ cups water

1 ½ cups toasted coconut flakes

MIX TOGETHER cake mix and water on low until moistened. Slowly increase speed until batter is fluffy and light.

SCOOP BATTER into paper liners, filling ¾ full.

BAKE AT 350 degrees for 20–25 minutes or until cake is light and golden in color. Remove from oven and cool on a wire rack.

MEANWHILE, PLACE coconut flakes on a cookie sheet, spreading out in a single layer. Bake at 400 degrees, checking every minute. It will only take about 2–4 minutes. The coconut will become fragrant and brown very easily. Set aside to cool.

FROST CUPCAKES with vanilla buttercream frosting and top with toasted coconut.

SERVES
18-20

FROSTING SUGGESTIONS
Vanilla Buttercream

Bridal Party
with Vanilla Buttercream

Bridal Party

This cupcake is so pretty and delicate. Little edible pansies liven up this cake and make it special and unforgettable. You can paint a small amount of water (with a small paint brush) on the petals of the flower and dust with sugar crystals to give it an extra-special touch.

1 box white cake mix

3 eggs

1 cup milk or sour cream

1 tsp. vanilla, lemon, or almond extract

edible flowers

MIX TOGETHER cake mix, eggs, milk or sour cream, and extract.

SCOOP BATTER into paper liners, filling ¾ full.

BAKE AT 350 degrees for 15–18 minutes or until cakes are light golden brown and spring back when lightly touched. Remove from oven and cool completely on a wire rack.

FROST WHEN cooled. Garnish with edible flowers.

SERVES
18-20

FROSTING SUGGESTIONS
White Chocolate Mousse • Vanilla Buttercream • Whipped Cream • Cream Cheese

Ginger Carrot Cake
with Orange Cream Cheese Frosting

Ginger Carrot Cake

My sister said if I were to make a cupcake cookbook, I must include a really good carrot cake recipe. Sis, this one's for you!

1 box carrot cake mix

3 eggs

1 cup milk

1 tsp. cinnamon

1 tsp. vanilla extract

1 tsp. ginger

1 cup raisins (optional)

1 cup chopped walnuts (optional)

MIX TOGETHER cake mix, eggs, milk, cinnamon, vanilla, and ginger. Add raisins and nuts if desired.

SCOOP BATTER into paper liners, filling ¾ full.

BAKE AT 350 degrees for 15–18 minutes or until cake springs back when lightly touched. Remove from oven and cool completely.

TOP WITH desired frosting. To garnish, sprinkle lightly with ground cinnamon.

SERVES
18-20

• • • • • • • • • • • • • • • • • • •

FROSTING SUGGESTIONS
Cream Cheese • Orange Cream Cheese • Vanilla Buttercream

Independence
Vanilla Cream
with Whipped Cream

Independence Vanilla Cream

These little cakes make a great dessert for a Fourth of July barbecue or any gathering during the summertime.

1 box white cake mix

3 eggs

1 cup milk

1 tsp. vanilla extract

strawberries, blueberries, or raspberries for garnish (fresh or frozen)

MIX TOGETHER cake mix, eggs, milk, and vanilla.

SCOOP BATTER into paper liners, filling ¾ full.

BAKE AT 350 degrees for 15–18 minutes or until cakes are light golden brown. Remove from pan and allow cupcakes to cool on a wire rack.

FROST GENEROUSLY and spoon fresh or frozen berries over the top just before serving.

SERVES 18-20

• •

FROSTING SUGGESTIONS
Whipped Cream • White Chocolate Mousse

Cinnamon Spice Buttermilk

This cupcake is sweet and spicy, with a little tang from the buttermilk. The perfect tastes of fall, or a special treat anytime.

1 box spice cake mix

3 eggs

1 cup buttermilk

2 tsp. vanilla extract

1 tsp. cinnamon

MIX TOGETHER all ingredients.

SCOOP BATTER into paper liners, filling ¾ full.

BAKE AT 350 degrees for 15–18 minutes or until cakes are light golden brown. Remove from oven and cool completely on a wire rack.

FROST WITH desired frosting.

SERVES
18-20

FROSTING SUGGESTIONS
Cream Cheese • Orange Cream Cheese • Vanilla Buttercream

Donut Cupcake

Sweet donuts are the ultimate treat. Can you ever eat just one? These cupcakes have endless possibilities for frosting. Berries or whipped cream sweeten these little cakes even more.

1 box yellow cake mix

2 eggs

1 cup milk

1 (4-oz.) pkg. instant vanilla pudding mix (powder only)

¼ cup mashed potatoes (can use instant)

1 tsp. vanilla extract

MIX TOGETHER all ingredients.

SCOOP BATTER into paper liners, filling ¾ full.

BAKE AT 350 degrees for 18–20 minutes or until cake springs back when lightly touched. Remove from oven and allow to cool on a wire rack.

COOL COMPLETELY before frosting.

SERVES
18-20

• • • • • • • • • • • • • • • • • •

FROSTING SUGGESTIONS
Caramel Cream • Vanilla Buttercream • Chocolate Buttercream

French Toast
with Maple Buttercream

French Toast

Yes, French toast cupcakes with bacon on top. Really, please trust me on this one. It may be my favorite cupcake so far. It's the best of both worlds—savory and sweet.

BONUS RECIPE!

1 box white cake mix

3 eggs

1 cup half-and-half

1 tsp. nutmeg

1 tsp. cinnamon

1 tsp. vanilla extract

½ lb. cooked bacon, cooled and either crumbled or cut into 2-inch strips

MIX TOGETHER cake mix, eggs, half-and-half, nutmeg, cinnamon, and vanilla extract. Batter will be thick.

SCOOP BATTER into paper liners, filling ¾ full.

BAKE AT 350 degrees for 15–18 minutes. Remove cupcakes from the oven and cool completely.

FROST WITH Maple Buttercream frosting and garnish with cooked and cooled bacon.

SERVES 18-20

• •

FROSTING SUGGESTIONS
Maple Buttercream

Ice Cream Sandwich

Ice Cream Sandwich

Cake and ice cream go hand in hand. Mixing these two together is a no-nonsense approach to dessert. You can have your cake and eat your ice cream too!

1 box white or chocolate cake mix

3 eggs

1 cup milk

1 tsp. vanilla extract

2 cups ice cream, your favorite flavor

MIX TOGETHER cake mix, eggs, milk, and vanilla.

SCOOP BATTER into paper liners, filling ¾ full.

BAKE AT 350 degrees for 15–18 minutes or until cake springs back when lightly touched. Remove from oven and allow to cool completely on a wire rack.

WHEN COOLED, remove the wrapper and cut the cupcake in half horizontally. Scoop your ice cream onto the bottom layer of cupcake. Top with other half.

FREEZE FOR 30 minutes to 1 hour to harden the ice cream.

FROST JUST before serving.

SERVES
18-20

FROSTING SUGGESTIONS
Chocolate Buttercream • Vanilla Buttercream • Peanut Butter

Candy Cane
with Vanilla Buttercream

Candy Cane

Make these for any Christmas gathering and please your friends and family. The white chocolate chunks and crushed peppermint candy add to the taste and texture of the little cake.

1 box white cake mix

3 eggs

1 cup milk

1 tsp. vanilla extract

1 recipe vanilla buttercream frosting

1 cup white chocolate chunks for garnish

peppermint candy for garnish

MIX TOGETHER cake mix, eggs, milk, and vanilla.

SCOOP BATTER into paper liners, filling ¾ full.

BAKE AT 350 degrees for 15–18 minutes or until cakes are light golden brown. Remove from oven and cool completely on a wire rack.

FROST WITH vanilla buttercream frosting and top generously with white chocolate chunks and crushed peppermint candies.

SERVES
18-20

• • • • • • • • • • • • • • • • • •

FROSTING SUGGESTIONS
Vanilla Buttercream

Pecan Pie

Can you taste this one already? Your mouth is watering, and you're thinking of the last time you ate this wonderful pie. Your next memory should be eating this delightful version, cupcake style. Come on, it's really simple!

1 box butter pecan cake mix

1 cup whole milk

1 cube butter, softened

5 eggs

1 tsp. vanilla extract

¾ cup dark corn syrup

¼ cup packed brown sugar

1½ cups roasted pecans, chopped or halved

MIX TOGETHER cake mix, milk, butter, 3 eggs, and vanilla. Pour about 2 tablespoons into paper liners.

IN A separate bowl, mix together corn syrup, brown sugar, chopped pecans, and 2 eggs. Divide nut mixture evenly among all the cupcakes, about 1 spoonful each. Scoop batter into paper liners, filling ¾ full.

SERVES 18-20

BAKE AT 350 degrees for 18–20 minutes or until cake springs back when lightly touched. Allow cakes to cool completely before serving. This allows the filling to set. If you don't want to frost, dust with powdered sugar and serve with a side of whipped cream.

• • • • • • • • • • • • • • • • • •

FROSTING SUGGESTIONS
Chocolate Buttercream • Vanilla Buttercream • Whipped Cream

Red Velvet Valentine

Make this special little cake for the ones you love. Pack it in their lunch or deliver it to work. What a great surprise! They will know you care and are thinking of them.

1 box red velvet cake mix

3 eggs

1 (8-oz.) pkg. cream cheese

1 cup milk

1 tsp. vanilla extract

heart-shaped foil liners

chocolate shavings or chunks for garnish

MIX TOGETHER cake mix, eggs, cream cheese, milk, and vanilla.

SCOOP BATTER into heart-shaped foil liners, filling ¾ full.

BAKE AT 350 degrees for 15–18 minutes or until cakes are light golden brown. Remove from oven and cool completely on a wire rack.

FROST AND garnish with chocolate shavings or chunks.

SERVES
18-20

• • • • • • • • • • • • • • • • •

FROSTING SUGGESTIONS
Chocolate Ganache • Chocolate Mousse • Chocolate Buttercream • Whipped Cream

Root Beer Float
with Root Beer Buttercream

Root Beer Float

My father-in-law loved a good glass of root beer. When he started saying we didn't need to buy him anything for Christmas or his birthday, someone would always give him a duffle bag of root beer—a three-month supply. This cupcake is in honor of him!

1 white cake mix

1 cup root beer

1 recipe vanilla buttercream

1 tsp. root beer flavoring

MIX TOGETHER cake mix and root beer.

SCOOP BATTER into paper liners, filling ¾ full.

BAKE AT 350 degrees for 15–18 minutes or until cake springs back when lightly touched. Remove from pan and allow cupcakes to cool on a wire rack.

IN A separate bowl, mix buttercream frosting and root beer flavoring. Frost cooled cupcakes.

SERVES
18-20

FROSTING SUGGESTIONS
Root Beer Buttercream

Harvest Pumpkin

My father tasted the combination of chocolate and butterscotch chips in a pumpkin cookie. This treat will surprise your taste buds and get you ready for fall.

1 box spice cake mix

1 cup pumpkin puree

2 eggs

½ cup milk

1 tsp. vanilla extract

1 cup chocolate chips

1 cup butterscotch chips

MIX TOGETHER all ingredients.

SCOOP BATTER into paper liners, filling ¾ full.

BAKE AT 350 degrees for 15–18 minutes or until cakes are light golden brown. Remove from the oven and cool completely on a wire rack.

SERVES
18-20

• •

FROSTING SUGGESTIONS

Chocolate Ganache • Chocolate Buttercream • Cream Cheese • Vanilla Buttercream

Gingerbread Cookie
with Cream Cheese Frosting

Gingerbread Cookie

Nothing says it's autumn better than a good gingerbread cookie. Now, nothing says it better than a gingerbread cookie cupcake!

1 box spice cake mix

3 eggs

⅓ cup molasses

⅓ cup oil

½ cup milk

MIX TOGETHER all ingredients.

SCOOP BATTER into paper liners, filling ¾ full.

BAKE AT 350 degrees for 15–18 minutes or until the cake springs back when lightly touched.

FROST WHEN cooled.

SERVES
18-20

FROSTING SUGGESTIONS
Cream Cheese • Orange Cream Cheese

Churro

with Whipped Cream

Churro

Every time I eat a churro, I think of Disneyland. Churros are warm, chewy, and covered with cinnamon and sugar. These cupcakes are best served warm.

1 box white cake mix

3 eggs

1 cup sour cream

1 tsp. vanilla extract

¾ cup sugar

2 Tbsp. cinnamon

4 Tbsp. butter, melted

MIX TOGETHER cake mix, eggs, sour cream, and vanilla. Put 2 tablespoons of batter in each paper liner.

IN A separate bowl, combine sugar and cinnamon. Stir until combined well. Sprinkle 1 teaspoon sugar mixture on top of cake batter. Top with remaining batter and fill ¾ full.

BAKE AT 350 degrees for 15–18 minutes or until cake springs back when lightly touched. Remove from oven and set aside.

WITH A pastry brush or spoon, brush melted butter on top of cupcakes. Sprinkle remaining sugar mix, dividing evenly among all cupcakes.

SERVES
18-20

• • • • • • • • • • • • • • • • • • • •

FROSTING SUGGESTIONS
Whipped Cream

Birthday Candles
with Vanilla Buttercream

Birthday Candles

When my children talk about these cupcakes, their faces light up.
My son asked, "When can we blow them out?"

I recipe of your favorite cupcake (18–24, baked and cooled)

I recipe vanilla buttercream frosting

I bag Life Savers

I box colored candles

sprinkles

FROST COOLED cupcakes with buttercream frosting. Center a Life Saver on top.

PLACE A candle through the center of the Life Saver.

USE SPRINKLES to garnish and add more color.

SERVES
18-24

• • • • • • • • • • • • • • • • •

FROSTING SUGGESTIONS
Vanilla Buttercream

Bird's Nest

This is a fun way to display Easter eggs for a party. You can even place a toothpick with a nametag in each cupcake to personalize the cupcakes or use them for place settings.

1 recipe of your favorite cupcake (18–24, baked and cooled)

1 recipe chocolate buttercream frosting

2 cups grated chocolate

1 bag chocolate egg candy

GENEROUSLY FROST cupcakes with chocolate buttercream frosting.

TOP WITH a small handful of grated chocolate (enough to cover the frosting), making a small rim around the edge of the cupcake.

PLACE 3 chocolate eggs in the center of the "nest" of grated chocolate.

SERVES
18-24

Birthday Presents

Use this breathtaking display at the next birthday party you attend. Presents are even better when you can eat them too!

1 recipe of your favorite cupcake (18–24, baked and cooled)

1 recipe vanilla buttercream frosting

18–24 square marshmallows (found in a specialty candy shop)

sprinkles

colored sugar

small bowl of water

paintbrush

vine-style licorice for ribbon

PAINT A small amount of water on each marshmallow square. Roll in colored sugar to coat. Set aside to dry.

WRAP EACH marshmallow present with licorice and tie in a loose knot or bow. Set marshmallows aside.

FROST CUPCAKES with buttercream frosting and top with sprinkles. Set finished marshmallow on top or off to the side, depending on your preference.

SERVES
18-24

Butterfly

Butterflies are magical. This arrangement is fast and easy, and it only takes a few minutes to prepare—and even fewer to decorate!

2 recipes of your favorite cupcake (36–48, baked and cooled)

2 recipes vanilla buttercream frosting

2 colors decorating sugars (i.e., dark pink and light pink or lavender and pink)

green sprinkles or sugar

black vine licorice for antennae

large platter (upside down cookie sheet works really well)

    for cupcakes to be decorated and presented on

FROST CUPCAKES. Cover 5 cupcakes with green sugar or sprinkles to make your butterfly body. Place in a single layer on the middle of the platter. The top cupcake will be your head. Place the black licorice (2-inch length) through the side of the paper liner. You may need to cut a slit in the paper to fit the licorice in to make the antennae.

SERVES 36–48

DIVIDE REMAINING cupcakes evenly. Cover half with one color of sugar and the rest with the second color. Choose a color and make a larger outline or a large half circle for the top wing on one side and repeat on the other side. Use the second colored cupcakes for the smaller wings, repeating the same process. Fill in any holes with remaining cupcakes.

Candy Bar Party

This cupcake can be tailored to all those who attend a party. You can use it as a get-to-know-you game. Each guest chooses the candy bar that best describes him and places it on a cupcake without others seeing. The other guests then try to guess which cupcake belongs to which guest. The person who claims the cupcake has to tell why the candy bar best describes him.

1 recipe of your favorite cupcake (18–24, baked and cooled)

1 recipe vanilla buttercream frosting

1 pkg. mini candy bars

FROST COOLED cupcakes. You can either place the whole mini candy bar on the top, or stick it in the center, leaving some showing. You can also chop the candy bar into smaller pieces and sprinkle them on top.

SERVES
18-24

Dinosaurs on
the Rocks
with Chocolate Buttercream

Dinosaurs on the Rocks

We all know a child who loves dinosaurs. These cupcakes are wonderful and easy to assemble. Plus, you can use the toy dinosaurs as party favors.

1 recipe of your favorite cupcake (18–24, baked and cooled)

1 recipe chocolate buttercream frosting

24 small plastic dinosaurs

1 bag rock candy

FROST CUPCAKES with chocolate frosting.

TOP WITH rock candy and place a plastic dinosaur on each cupcake.

SERVES
18-24

· ·

FROSTING SUGGESTIONS
Chocolate Buttercream

Caterpillar

A simple but very creative way to arrange cupcakes. You can even use smashed chocolate sandwich cookies to make the dirt the caterpillar rests on.

1 recipe of your favorite cupcake (18–24, baked and cooled)

1 recipe vanilla buttercream frosting

green food coloring

green sprinkles

1 bag stick pretzels for legs

black gel icing to make the eyes (or black jelly beans)

large platter (upside down cookie sheet works really well) for cupcakes

   to be decorated and presented on

COMBINE FROSTING and green food coloring and mix until icing is completely green. Frost cupcakes and cover with green sprinkles.

ARRANGE CUPCAKES in an "S" shape on your serving tray. Place 2 pretzels for the legs on each side of every cupcake. Use black gel icing or place black jelly beans on the head for the eyes.

SERVES
18-24

Christmas Tree

This is an easy way to get the kids involved with decorating and having a good time in the kitchen. It's never too early to start. Even my two-year-old can frost a cupcake—it's a masterpiece every time!

1 recipe of your favorite cupcake (18–24, baked and cooled)

1 recipe vanilla buttercream frosting

large platter (upside down cookie sheet works really well) for cupcakes
   to be decorated and presented on

green food coloring

assorted candy to decorate the frosted tree

MIX TOGETHER vanilla buttercream frosting and green food coloring.

FROST AND place the cupcakes in rows, starting with the bottom row of 7 cupcakes, then 6, 5, and so on, ending with 1.

PLACE ONE last cupcake at the center of the bottom for the trunk.

LET THE kids decorate the tree with all of the candy. This is a great job for them.

SERVES
18-24

• • • • • • • • • • • • • • • • •

FROSTING SUGGESTIONS
Whipped Cream

Easter Peeps

Nothing says Easter is close like a box of Peeps!

1 recipe of your favorite cupcake (18–24, baked and cooled)

1 recipe vanilla buttercream frosting

green food coloring

1 cup shredded coconut

3 medium pkgs. of bunny or chick Peeps

ADD 3–4 drops green food coloring to vanilla buttercream frosting and mix until combined. Set aside.

PUT COCONUT in a separate bowl and add 2–3 drops green food coloring, stirring until all coconut has turned green. Frost cupcakes generously.

WITH YOUR fingers, pat coconut onto moist frosting, making sure there are enough coats to make the coconut look like grass. Place a Peep in the center of the cupcake and serve on a platter.

SERVES
18-24

Flower Power

For springtime parties or to bring a bouquet of edible cupcake flowers to someone special, all you need are a few simple extra ingredients.

1 recipe of your favorite cupcake (18–24, baked and cooled)

1 recipe vanilla buttercream frosting

red and yellow food coloring

red and yellow sprinkles or crushed candy to garnish

large platter (upside down cookie sheet works really well) for flower cupcakes

   to be decorated and presented on

PLACE FROSTING in a large bowl, minus about ¾ cup. Place ¾ cup frosting in a separate bowl. Add 1–3 drops yellow food coloring to ¾ cup frosting. Stir well until yellow food coloring has become even. Set aside.

FOR THE larger amount of frosting, place 2–3 drops red food coloring and stir well until red coloring has become even. Set aside.

USING YOUR offset spatula, frost yellow buttercream frosting onto 3 cupcakes. Place them spaced apart (for the petals of the flower to be placed around the center) on the platter.

FROST REMAINING cupcakes with red frosting. Place the red frosted cupcakes around the yellow ones.

ADD SPRINKLES and embellish any way you'd like.

SERVES
18-24

Banana Split

Banana Split

This cupcake is so much fun to make, but even more fun to eat.

1 recipe of your favorite cupcake (18–24, baked and cooled)

1 recipe chocolate ganache

6 bananas, sliced

maraschino cherries

1 recipe whipped cream

chopped nuts (optional)

TOP CUPCAKES with chocolate ganache and sliced bananas, dividing them evenly among all the cupcakes. Finish with cherries, whipped cream, and nuts (optional).

SERVES
18-24

Creepy Spider

This decorated cupcake is sure to give your little goblins a fright on Halloween night!

1 recipe of your favorite cupcake (18–24, baked and cooled)

1 recipe chocolate frosting

24 chocolate with chocolate cream–filled cookies

black vine licorice

FROST COOKIES with chocolate ganache.

CUT 1½–2-inch pieces of licorice and stick in the sides of each of the cookies for the spider legs.

PLACE A leggy cookie on the center of each frosted cupcake.

SERVES
18-24

Easter Egg Basket

Kids will love decorating these before Easter. This is a great hands-on project for any baker-in-training.

1 recipe of your favorite cupcake (18–24, baked and cooled)

green food coloring

1 recipe vanilla buttercream frosting

1 cup shredded coconut

24 pipe cleaners in a variety of colors

candy eggs for decorating

ADD 3–4 drops green food coloring to vanilla buttercream frosting and mix until combined. Set aside.

IN A separate bowl, add 2–3 drops green food coloring to coconut, stirring until all coconut has turned green. Frost cupcakes generously.

WITH YOUR fingers, pat coconut onto moist frosting, making sure there are enough coats to make the coconut look like grass. Place your pipe cleaner on opposite sides of the cupcake, making a handle. Put candy in the center so it will look like a basket of goodies.

SERVES
18-24

• • • • • • • • • • • • • • • • •

FROSTING SUGGESTIONS
Vanilla Buttercream

Fudge Sundae Cone

This is a fun twist on serving a cupcake. Try it sometime when you are in the mood for an ice cream cone. Just add the cupcakes!

vanilla ice cream

1 recipe of your favorite chocolate cupcake (18–24, baked and cooled)

24 ice cream cones

1 recipe chocolate ganache

PLACE A scoop of ice cream on each cupcake. Top with a cone, slightly tipped to the side.

DRIZZLE GENEROUSLY with chocolate ganache.

SERVES
18-24

Holiday Wreath

Another fun decorating idea where the kids can help.

green food coloring

1 recipe vanilla buttercream frosting

1 recipe of your favorite cupcake (18–24, baked and cooled)

large platter (upside down cookie sheet works really well) for cupcakes
    to be decorated and presented on

1 bag red candy or chocolate-covered cherries (red shell)

red vine licorice

MIX TOGETHER green food coloring and buttercream frosting. Frost cupcakes and arrange in a circle, 2 rows deep.

TOP WITH red candy or chocolate-covered cherries, placing several on each cupcake. Make a bow using licorice and place at the bottom, centered or slightly off to the side.

SERVES
18-24

• • • • • • • • • • • • • • • • • • • •

FROSTING SUGGESTIONS
Whipped Cream

Cupcake Flower
Bouquet

Cupcake Flower Bouquet

I came up with this idea for a segment on Studio 5. What a great centerpiece for any party! It's simply stunning.

BONUS RECIPE!

Rock or brick to weigh down the basket

1 basket or pot with a 6-inch radius

Glue

6-inch floral foam or floral ball

Assortment of silk or fresh flowers

Craft sticks

6–8 regular cupcakes, frosted

6–8 mini cupcakes, frosted

Floral moss

PLACE THE brick or rock in the bottom of the basket or pot. Secure with glue if needed. Place a 6-inch foam ball into the pot and secure around the edges with glue. Begin placing flowers, working from the bottom up, leaving some room for the occasional cupcake to be placed. Place the craft stick in the spots you have for the cupcakes. Then, using a sharp paring knife, slice a small slit in the bottom of the cupcake. Secure the cupcakes into the craft sticks. Repeat until all spaces have been filled and bouquet looks full. Fill in any empty holes with moss.

SERVES
12-16

• • • • • • • • • • • • • • • • • • •

HELPFUL HINTS

Freezing or cooling the cupcakes is a great idea. Cupcakes are more likely to stay put when frozen. Keep the frosting light and simple. That way the cupcakes won't topple over. Use the flowers to help stabilize the cupcakes as you work your way around the foam.

Little Sheep

Little Bo Peep won't lose all her sheep until it's time to eat these cupcakes!

1 recipe of your favorite cupcake (18–24, baked and cooled)

1 recipe vanilla buttercream frosting

1 bag large marshmallows

1 bag miniature marshmallows

toothpicks

black gel icing in a tube

FROST CUPCAKES with buttercream icing.

PLACE 1 large marshmallow on its side near the edge of each cupcake. Secure with more icing if needed.

PLACE MINI marshmallows on cupcakes, small sides down, and cover entire top of cake. (This is the sheep's wool.)

BREAK TOOTHPICKS in half and secure a mini marshmallow on one end of each toothpick. Place these toothpicks (one on each side) through the top of the large marshmallow for the ears. With the black gel icing, make two dots for the eyes.

SERVES 18-24

Lucky Green

St. Patrick's Day is all about celebrating with friends and family. Serve these cupcakes for dessert.

1 recipe vanilla buttercream frosting

green food coloring

plastic sandwich bag

1 recipe of your favorite cupcake (18–24, baked and cooled)

green sprinkles or sugar

PLACE FROSTING and 2–3 drops food coloring in bowl and mix well. Scoop several spoonfuls of frosting inside bag. Squeeze all the air out and seal. Cut off bottom tip of plastic bag with a pair of scissors.

ON THE top of the cupcake, trace the shape of a four-leaf clover with the frosting. Now, fill in the clover with the frosting. The clover will not cover every inch of the cupcake. Put desired amount of sprinkles on top.

SERVES
18-24

New Year's Celebration

With the special touch of sparkler candles, this cupcake makes any party sizzle!

1 box confetti cake mix

3 eggs

1 cup milk

1 tsp. vanilla

sprinkles

1 recipe vanilla buttercream frosting

sparkler candles

MIX TOGETHER cake mix, eggs, milk, and vanilla.

SCOOP BATTER into paper liners, filling ¾ full.

BAKE AT 350 degrees for 15–18 minutes or until cake springs back when lightly touched. Allow cupcakes to cool completely.

IN A separate bowl, combine sprinkles and buttercream frosting. Frost cupcakes generously and place a sparkler candle on top. Light candles just before serving.

SERVES
18-24

Pumpkin

Celebrate the harvest season with this festive cupcake.

red and yellow food coloring

1 recipe vanilla buttercream frosting

1 recipe of your favorite cupcake (18–24, baked and cooled)

black gel icing

candy corn

green gel icing

IN A large mixing bowl, combine food coloring and frosting, adding 3–4 drops yellow food coloring and 1–2 red to get the color of orange you want.

FROST CUPCAKES with orange icing. Draw lines for grooves of the pumpkin with black icing. Place candy corn for eyes, mouth, and nose. Be creative! Use green gel icing to make a small stem at the top of the pumpkin if you desire.

SERVES
18-24

Team Edward
with Vanilla Buttercream

Team Edward

Yes, I know. I've become one of them. . . . At least I've made a fantastic Team Edward cupcake, worthy of any vampire lover.

BONUS RECIPE!

1 box red velvet cake mix

3 eggs

¼ cup butter, softened

½ cup sour cream

1 tsp. vanilla extract

white edible glitter or sugar

MIX TOGETHER cake mix, eggs, butter, sour cream, and vanilla extract. Batter will be thick.

SCOOP BATTER into paper liners, filling ¾ full.

BAKE AT 350 degrees for 15–18 minutes. Remove from oven and cool completely.

FROST COOLED cupcakes with Vanilla Buttercream frosting and top generously with white edible glitter or sprinkles.

SERVES 18-24

• • • • • • • • • • • • • • • • • •

FROSTING SUGGESTIONS
Vanilla Buttercream

Team Jacob

with Chocolate Ganache

Team Jacob

I can't have a cupcake for the vampires and leave out the werewolves, right? Here's a rich dark chocolate cake, perfect for Team Jacob. You know who you are.

BONUS RECIPE!

1 box Swiss chocolate cake mix or dark chocolate cake mix

3 eggs

1 cup half-and-half

1 tsp. vanilla extract

1 recipe chocolate ganache

1 cup grated dark chocolate

MIX TOGETHER cake mix, eggs, half-and-half, and vanilla extract. Batter will be thick.

SCOOP BATTER into paper liners, filling ¾ full.

BAKE AT 350 degrees for 15–18 minutes. Remove from oven and cool completely.

FROST WITH Chocolate Ganache and top with grated dark chocolate.

SERVES 18-24

FROSTING SUGGESTIONS
Chocolate Ganache

Rainbow

At the end of every storm, there is always a rainbow somewhere.

2 recipes of your favorite cupcake (36–48, baked and cooled)

2 recipes vanilla buttercream frosting

4 small bowls

red, yellow, green, and blue food coloring

large platter (upside down cookie sheet works really well) for cupcakes to be decorated

   and presented on

PUT 1 CUP frosting into each bowl. Leave the remaining frosting in the mixing bowl. Add 3–5 drops of red food coloring into the mixing bowl and combine. Add yellow food coloring to one smaller bowl, green food coloring to another, and blue to another small bowl. Leave one bowl with white or plain frosting to top the "cloud" cupcakes.

FROST 14 CUPCAKES with red frosting and place in a half circle on the serving platter. Frost 11 cupcakes with yellow frosting and place them in a row, following the outline of the red. Frost 9 green cupcakes and repeat the pattern next to the yellow. Then follow with 6 of the blue.

FROST REMAINING cupcakes with white frosting and place on either end of the rainbow, making them look like clouds.

SERVES
36-48

Spring Garden

This is a great display of cupcakes for any spring birthday or shower. You can use this arrangement for your centerpiece or as individual place settings for nametags. Your friends' faces will light up if you bring several on a plate to say "thanks" or "you're great!"

1 recipe of your favorite cupcake (18–24, baked and cooled)

1 recipe chocolate buttercream frosting

10–12 chocolate sandwich cookies, crushed into fine crumbs

1–2 (16-oz.) bag(s) gumdrops

1 box toothpicks

1 (16-oz.) bag gummy worms

FROST COOLED cupcakes with chocolate frosting and top with cookie crumbs. This is your "dirt."

SPEAR 24 GUMDROPS with toothpicks, using the bottom of the toothpicks to place into the cupcakes to secure. Set aside.

BREAK SEVERAL toothpicks in half to make anchors for your flower petals. Cut the rest of the gumdrops in half, making the shape of a flower petal. Spear a halved gumdrop, securing with the toothpick and leaving space to secure to flower. Repeat until all petals have been secured.

TO ASSEMBLE the flowers, place the halved gumdrops around the center of the whole gumdrop. Place the long toothpick into the cupcake "dirt." Place 1–3 flowers on each cupcake. Place a gummy worm, if desired, at the bottom of the dirt.

SERVES
18-24

Picnic Cake in a Jar

This recipe is fun and different. Besides giving you your own glass to eat out of, it's creative and great to transport on a picnic or camping trip.

butter

6 (1-pint) canning jars

1 recipe of your favorite cupcake (batter only, not baked yet!)

cookie sheet

6 canning jar lids and rims in boiling water

fruit or chocolate ganache

BUTTER EACH jar well, being careful not to get anything on the rims. Pour 1 cup batter into each jar, wiping off the top if spills occur.

PLACE JARS evenly on a cookie sheet and bake at 350 degrees for 30–35 minutes. Remove from oven.

USING A hot pad or towel to protect your hands, immediately place a hot rim and lid on each pint jar, sealing tightly. Then turn upside down and rest on a towel.

SERVES
18-24

ALLOW TO cool and seal.

WHEN READY to serve, top each cake with fruit or chocolate ganache. These cakes will keep in the refrigerator unopened for up to 3 weeks.

The Icing on the Little Cakes

Whipped Cream

You can choose stiff or loose peaks, depending on your preference. Stiff peaks are easier to frost and stand tall to make designs.

2 cups heavy whipping cream

¼–½ cup powdered sugar (depending on preference)

POUR CREAM into large mixing bowl and start mixing at low speed. Gradually increase speed until cream thickens and soft peaks form.

TURN OFF mixer and add sugar. Start slowly again—no messes today! Beat until stiff peaks form.

THE STIFFER the cream, the easier it is to frost the cupcakes. Keep refrigerated.

Cream Cheese

Sophisticated taste and an even better look. This frosting is glossy and smooth.

8 oz. cream cheese, softened

½ cup butter, softened

3¾ cups powdered sugar

1 tsp. vanilla extract

BEAT TOGETHER cream cheese and butter until smooth and light.

STOP MIXER and add sugar and vanilla.

START MIXER on low and gradually increase the speed until frosting is fluffy. Keep frosting refrigerated.

Vanilla Buttercream

A classic base to so many different recipes, this frosting will become a favorite staple to your baking.

8 Tbsp. (1 stick) butter, room temperature

3¾ cups powdered sugar, sifted

3–4 Tbsp. milk or cream

2 tsp. vanilla extract

PLACE BUTTER in a large mixing bowl. Beat until light and fluffy, about 30 seconds. Stop beating before adding sugar to avoid a large mess.

ADD SUGAR. 3 tablespoons milk or cream, and vanilla extract. Beat frosting starting on slow, increasing your speed until frosting is nice and creamy. Add up to 1 more tablespoon milk or cream if frosting is too thick.

Chocolate Buttercream

Rich, chocolaty, and smooth—this frosting is a classic!

8 Tbsp. (1 stick) butter, room temperature

⅓ cup cocoa

3¾ cups powdered sugar, sifted

3–4 Tbsp. milk or cream

2 tsp. vanilla extract

BEAT BUTTER in a large mixing bowl until light and fluffy, about 30 seconds. Stop mixer before adding cocoa to avoid a large mess.

ADD COCOA, sugar, 3 tablespoons milk or cream, and vanilla extract. Beat frosting starting on slow speed and add up to 1 more tablespoon milk or cream if frosting is too thick.

Caramel Cream

Holy cow! Caramel cream tastes great on any of the chocolate cupcakes too.

4 Tbsp. butter

¼ cup brown sugar

¼ cup dark brown sugar

2–3 Tbsp. whole milk

1 cup powdered sugar

1 tsp. vanilla extract

PLACE BUTTER and brown sugars in a medium skillet over medium heat. Stir and cook the mixture until it comes to a boil.

ADD MILK and bring the mixture back to a boil, stirring constantly.

REMOVE PAN from heat and add powdered sugar and vanilla. Beat mixture with a wooden spoon until smooth and creamy.

ALLOW THE cupcakes to cool slightly before frosting. Frosting will harden when cooled completely.

Chocolate Mousse

This frosting is light but rich in flavor.

1 recipe whipped cream
1 (4-oz) box chocolate pudding (powder only)

ADD CREAM to large mixing bowl and pour pudding powder on top. Fold chocolate gently into the cream without losing air from beaten cream.

FROST ONLY completely cooled cakes. Keep refrigerated.

Chocolate Ganache

Ganache. Just that word makes you think, "It's too difficult and time-consuming. How can I ever do this?" But, if you just try it once, you'll be hooked. It's the best way to impress.

1 cup heavy whipping cream

12 oz. semi-sweet chocolate chunks or chips

HEAT CREAM in a saucepan until it comes to a boil.

REMOVE FROM heat and pour over chocolate in a mixing bowl. Stir to mix together. You can pour it over your cakes warm or allow it to cool slightly and then spread it like frosting.

Lemon Cream

Lemons and cream. Did I say I have a favorite? Well, I should be honest—
every cupcake is pretty much my favorite.

2 cups heavy whipping cream

¼ – ½ cup powdered sugar (depending on preference)

1–2 tsp. lemon extract

1 Tbsp. grated lemon zest, finely chopped

POUR CREAM into large mixing bowl and begin to mix at low speed. Gradually increase speed until cream thickens and soft peaks form.

TURN OFF mixer and add sugar, lemon extract, and lemon zest. Start slowly again—no messes today!

BEAT UNTIL stiff peaks form. The stiffer the cream, the easier it is to frost the cupcakes. Keep refrigerated.

Peanut Butter

This frosting is my son's favorite. He said, "I would put this on anything, even pancakes!"

1 cup peanut butter (chunky or smooth—I prefer smooth)

½ cup butter, room temperature

2 cups powdered sugar

3–4 Tbsp. milk or cream

1 tsp. vanilla extract

COMBINE peanut butter and butter in a large bowl, mixing together until light and fluffy. Stop mixer before adding sugar.

ADD SUGAR, 3 tablespoons milk or cream, and vanilla. Start slow and mix together, gradually increasing the speed. Mix until smooth and creamy. Add 1 tablespoon milk or cream if frosting is too thick.

Chocolate Sour Cream

Deep, rich chocolate with a tangy zip adds depth and dimension to any choice of cupcakes.

8 Tbsp. (1 stick) butter, room temperature

3¾ cups powdered sugar, sifted

3–4 Tbsp. sour cream

¼ cup cocoa

PLACE BUTTER in large mixing bowl. Beat until light and fluffy, about 30 seconds. Stop the mixer before adding sugar to avoid a large mess.

ADD SUGAR and 3 tablespoons sour cream. Beat frosting, starting on low and increasing your speed until frosting is nice and creamy. If the frosting is too thick, add 1 more tablespoon sour cream, mixing thoroughly.

Orange Cream Cheese

Zesty and creamy are some of the best toppings to the perfect soft cupcake.

8 oz. cream cheese, softened

½ cup butter, softened

3¾ cups powdered sugar

1 tsp. orange extract

¼ cup frozen orange concentrate

BEAT TOGETHER cream cheese and butter until smooth and light. Stop mixer and add sugar, orange extract, and orange concentrate. Start mixer on slow and gradually increase the speed until frosting is fluffy.

FROST AND refrigerate.

Pink Lemonade Cream

Yummy! This frosting is sweet and tangy.

8 Tbsp. (1 stick) butter, room temperature

3¾ cups powdered sugar, sifted

3–4 Tbsp. milk or cream

1–2 drops red food coloring

2 tsp. lemon extract

PLACE BUTTER in large mixing bowl. Beat until light and fluffy, about 30 seconds. Stop the mixer before adding the sugar to avoid a large mess.

ADD SUGAR, 3 tablespoons milk or cream, food coloring, and lemon extract. Beat frosting starting on slow speed and increasing your speed until frosting is nice and creamy. Add up to 1 more tablespoon milk or cream if frosting is too thick.

Root Beer Buttercream

I couldn't make a root beer cupcake and not have root beer frosting to pair it with.

8 Tbsp. (1 stick) butter, room temperature

3¾ cups powdered sugar, sifted

3–4 Tbsp. milk or cream

1 tsp. root beer flavoring

PLACE BUTTER in a large mixing bowl. Beat until light and fluffy, about 30 seconds. Stop the mixer before adding sugar to avoid a large mess.

ADD SUGAR, 3 tablespoons milk or cream, and root beer flavoring. Beat frosting, starting on slow and increasing your speed until frosting is nice and creamy. Add up to 1 more tablespoon milk or cream if frosting is too thick.

White Chocolate Mint

The white chocolate chunks are a great addition to this frosting. The texture is outstanding.

8 Tbsp. (1 stick) butter, room temperature

3¾ cups powdered sugar, sifted

3–4 Tbsp. milk or cream

1 tsp. mint extract

1 cup white chocolate, finely chopped

PLACE BUTTER in a large mixing bowl. Beat until light and fluffy, about 30 seconds. Stop mixer before adding sugar to avoid a large mess.

ADD SUGAR, 3 tablespoons milk or cream, and mint extract. Beat frosting starting on low, increasing your speed until frosting is nice and creamy. Add 1 cup finely chopped white chocolate into frosting. Add up to 1 more tablespoon of milk or cream if frosting is too thick.

White Chocolate Mousse

Soft and light with a hint of white chocolate flavor has made this frosting a favorite of my family.

1 recipe whipped cream

1 cup white chocolate chunks, melted and cooled

ADD CREAM to large mixing bowl. Fold chocolate gently into cream, without losing air from beaten cream.

FROST ONLY completely cooled cakes. Keep refrigerated.

Maple Buttercream

This frosting is great on just about anything.

2 sticks butter, softened

1 lb. powdered sugar

1½ tsp. maple flavoring

3 Tbsp. heavy cream or more if desired

IN A large mixer, beat butter until smooth. Add maple flavoring and cream. Slowly add powdered sugar and beat until light and fluffy. If needed, add more cream, 1 tablespoon at a time until desired consistency is achieved.

Recipe Index

About the Author

WENDY L. PAUL has been cooking and baking for many years. She enjoys writing new recipes and creating easy-to-make dinners and desserts. Her baking skills have been featured on numerous morning TV shows and news programs. When Wendy is working on a project—whether home improvement, a new recipe, or shopping at a craft store—she is truly happy. She is the bestselling author of *101 Gourmet Cupcakes in 10 Minutes* and *101 Gourmet Cookies for Everyone*. She and her family live in Utah, and oddly enough have a dog named Cupcake. For more information, visit her website at www.wendypaul creations.com.

About *the* Photographer

MARIELLE HAYES is a photographer based in the San Francisco Bay Area. When she is not behind the camera, she enjoys traveling and spending time with her friends and family. She resides in the Oakland Hills with her husband, daughter, and Boston Terrier dog.